C000142124

Nicole Luck

Energy of Uniqueness

novum ▲ premium

This book is also
available as
e-book.

www.novum-publishing.co.uk

© 2021 novum publishing

ISBN 978-3-903861-79-4
Editing: Ashleigh Brassfield, DipEdit
Cover photo: Pitris | Dreamstime.com
Cover design, layout & typesetting:
novum publishing

www.novum-publishing.co.uk

Index

Entrance

Enter the kingdom of light.
For there you will find peace and harmony.
For that is your soul.
The entity.
The energy that flows thru all of us.
To be unique.
For we are unique.
For that is the beauty of being alive not only within but all
around us.
The soul.
It is a combination of time, space and more.
The soul.
Oh, the soul.
For without you, where would we be.
Everywhere and nowhere.

Hollow

Do you feel it.
I can't explain it.
It's in the atmosphere.
Time.
Space.
The energy that flows thru me.
Hollow.
How to explain this feeling.
For even I cannot put it into words.
I just sense it.
Its like the universe is holding its breath.
In anticipation.
For what?

Verge

We are on the verge of many new exciting things.
The verge where humans begin to look inside.
For the soul is wanting to expand.
For the time has come, has it not?
Can you feel it?
When you walk in nature, you can feel the earth beneath
your feet.
The energy that flows thru constantly.
For the soul is on the verge of wanting to bring forth a
message.
Oh, I can't wait what it is for something wonderful.
Be patient and be open.

Skilful

To be skilful.
Requires skill in being able to convey what you are
wanting to say.
To have that skill to lead.
For not all have that skill which leaders need.
For there are those among us who have the courage to be
strong.
For they have learned the art of being among many.
For it takes patience, a calmness within, a sense of justice to
all mankind and more.
To be skilful.
Do you have the necessary skills?

Convey

To convey the truth.
For many have the inability to do so.
To be upfront.
For it takes courage.
Courage to be honest.
For humans have a difficulty in accepting the truth.
Even thou they like to be told the truth then the opposite.
But often times they prefer to be lied to for it helps to ease
the pain.
Am I wrong to say this?
I don't know.
Its just a feeling I have.
For I would prefer to be told the truth then to be lied to.
You?

Inability

That inability to be truthful.
For there are creatures in today's world who would rather blame others then themselves.
That inability to look within and sort thru their life experiences.
For once they have done that, for it takes many months or years, to heal.
For the soul is patient.
But the mind is unable or unwilling to compromise.
For its stubborn.
But in time, it concedes and realizes its mistake.
Oh, humans, try and be more in tune to yourself.

Accountable

To be held accountable.
To say one thing and do the opposite.
For it means to be responsible for things when you don't
always want to be.
There are those that are good in being responsible.
For they love to be in charge.
Meaning they thrive in being in control of the situation.
That is good for we need more humans that are
accountable for their actions.
For many humans just follow and not think.
Oh, to be human!

Thrive

To thrive.
Humans thrive.
Nature thrives.
I wonder who will thrive the longest.
Who has the capability to survive?
To evolve.
For humans are organic and so is nature.
But the soul is energy.
I think we can agree that it's the energy that will thrive.
For it flows thru us, nature and the universe.
It's all around us.
Oh, how beautiful nature is.

Wonder

Life is a wonder.
Is it not?
To see before you a beautiful cherry blossom tree.
All bright and pink.
For spring is around the corner.
To feel the crispy air blow into your face.
Ruffling your hair as you look at the beautiful tree in front
of you.
For everything around you is rather dull.
Oh, how I look forward to spring for the beautiful flowers
will explode in eccentric colours like a rainbow in the sky.

Guidance

We all need a bit of guidance in our lives.
For we don't know everything.
For its nice to have good friends to talk things thru
especially as we evolve within ourselves.
And as we become one with the soul, we need to be in
balance within ourselves and the mind.
For the mind needs time to find that balance of adjustment.
For its all new.
But its open to the guidance of the soul.
So, thank you!

Masquerade

Humans masquerade as if there is no tomorrow.
To put on a show for all to see that they are not afraid.
Oh, what a masquerade life is.
For everyday its something unique.
For many humans life is a show.
For to be otherwise means to show the world who they truly are.
Many do not have the courage to be, but you need not be afraid.
Just trust that all will be well.
Oh, to be human yet more.

Energizer

Explosive energies these little dogs.
Sprinting down the path.
Like they know they are in trouble.
For when the master calls, they must comply.
Whether they want to or not.
For half the time their noses are busy sniffing the grass.
Looking for something exciting to chow on or any message
that some other dog might have left behind.
Oh, the life of a dog.
All so cute.
Full of energy and spark.
Such elegance while they race across the park.
All the while, their master yelling for them, at them or
with them.
Oh, the game is on between master and dog.

Worth

Why do humans feel as thou they are not worth anything?
What makes one say that?
The underachiever.
The one's who feel they have not succeeded in anything.
We all are achievers.
No matter how minute you contribute to society.
Don't let others be the ones to make you feel less.
Look inside for its there.
Waiting for you to be one with the soul.
For the soul will show you the way and be courageous.
No matter what!

Achiever

The achievers.
Who are they?
They are no more special then you or me.
They are human.
Are they not?
Some achieve because they work hard and still are not
happy.
Some achieve because they are born into that family.
Some achieve because they listen to their souls.
But we are all achievers no matter whether we are rich or
poor.
Its not what makes us who we are.
Does it?

Lifeless

Have you noticed humans have become lifeless?
Like they have given up on hope.
Why?
Such sadness to see for it makes me want to know why?
What makes you feel so lifeless?
What has brought you to this point in life?
Why?
Don't let sadness get you down.
For there is so much beauty around you, is there not?

Silky

What beautiful silky black fur you have.
All so finely layered.
Each feather silkier than the next.
For you are a proud crow.
Strutting around immaculately.
Looking for grass to build your nest.
What magnificent creatures you are.
Each unique to the next.
How I love watching you in the park.
For you are an interesting bird to say the least.
For you are loners yet like to be around your family if need
be.

Plenty

There are plenty of cabs.
All waiting for customers.
No one is tempted.
Buses are nearly empty.
For people are scared.
Why?
All one has to do is take the necessary precautions and you
will be safe.
Oh, there are plenty of spaces.
London is so sparse to say the least.
It's a new era.
So, take care and be safe.

Stroll

To stroll thru the park.
Looking at the bare trees.
Each unique for its rather fascinating to say the least.
I find it a wonder that each tree has its own unique stance.
As thou they are putting on a show and waiting for
someone to watch.
To stroll thru the park watching the dogs run like mad
after the squirrel and looking disappointed when they can't.
To stroll thru the park under the warmth of the sun
thinking about nothing.
Just feeling the energy from the ground flowing thru you.
Oh, what a great day it was!

Grounded

To be grounded.
Means to be balanced.
Balanced between the mind and the soul.
For they are two yet one.
For to be grounded means to work together as a team.
For to be balanced not only within the soul but the mind must be calm as well.
To allow itself to be one with the soul.
For it's the soul that encourages the mind to let go of its constraints.
To trust and be open to other ideas.
That balance between one another.

Constraints

What constraints do humans have?
That the mind imposes upon oneself.
Is that because its been taught from a young age and then throughout one's lifetime of growth?
Those constraints that humans imposed upon themselves.
Are those constraints beneficial?
Do they help you in anyway?
Like the way you live or have these constraints caused more problems than necessary?
Oh, to be a human living on earth.

Uneasy

To have that uneasy feeling.
To know that things will be different for a while.
For humans are not used to being on their own.
For they like to be among others.
Where they do not have to be with oneself.
For when they are on their own, they become mad.
The four walls start to close in.
Fear not, for life will return to normal.
Just learn to be patient with oneself and you will be fine.

Walls

I can feel the walls closing in on me.
As this has become my new reality.
For life is uniquely different.
Many thousands of humans have been advised to stay
home.
To appease the virus so that no one gets sicker.
Oh, how the world has changed but not really.
For life goes on.
Just need to be more cautious.
But fear not for you can cope.
Trust yourself and be aware of your surroundings.

Close

Things are coming to a close.
Where life will become more meaningful.
For you will get to know yourself once and for all.
To become in tune with the soul.
For the soul is waiting ever so patient.
So close.
Where the mind and the soul become a unit.
One yet always separate.
For it means that you must trust each other.
And that is hard for the mind.
For the mind is what society has made it to be whereas the
soul is the energy that surrounds us.

Deserted

Oh, the streets of London have become deserted.
All of sudden people have realized that life has become serious.
To take heed.
For life has turned a corner.
That's good that its finally dawned.
For the species is at risk, is it not?
But it will eventually come back to normal, but no one knows for how long.
Take care my fellow humans.
All will be well.

Dawn

Oh, the dawn of a new day has begun.
Where one sees the sun rising ever so clearly.
The clouds giving way to the warm sun for its been chilly
at nights.
Oh, to watch the night become day.
To realize that spring is around the corner.
For winter has been strange this year.
Oh, dawn.
What an amazing time it is for it means one wakes up
earlier to see the sun rise while listening to the birds sing at
all hours of the day.

Dire

Humans are in dire need for a solution.
They will be lost without it.
But it will be alright.
Just trust yourself for that is the way forward.
For life goes on.
For your soul never dies.
It's the energy within you and around you.
You can feel it, can you not?
I know you humans always want to see but some things in life, just can't.
Otherwise, where is the mystery in that.

Race

Race against time.
Time to race.
Or not.
For time is consistent yet flexible.
For it flows thru all of us whether we are in a race or not.
Time.
Time will tell you who survives and who doesn't.
Life.
Don't be afraid for we never die, just our body.
And yet the body will be born again.
So, there is no race in time.
Just time!

Time

Time will tell.
How humans will react.
Will it not?
Time will tell.
How society as a whole will come together.
But it has been shown otherwise over and over again.
Time will tell.
For life is never straight forward.
Time will tell.
The situation will get worse before it gets better.
Time will tell.
But humans are strong.
Do not let fear win for we all have that inner strength
within us.

React

How one reacts often shows the stamina of will inside.
For to be chaotic shows one can't cope.
To be calm, an undeniable strength.
To laugh, not sure.
To chatter, nervous.
To be rude, aggressive out of fear.
So, take care before you react in a way that you might regret later.
Humans are a bred unto themselves, are they not?

Cope

This will be a time for humans to learn new things about themselves.
Life strategies.
For we know how to cope, we just forgot.
But humans are stronger than they know.
For its within.
The soul.
The soul will show you the way.
The soul that has infinite power.
The soul that is full of love, harmony, light and unbelievable strength.
Just look within and the soul will cope with you!

Strategies

What strategies have you come up with?
Many.
Yet when the time has come you will know what to do.
Some yes and some no.
Oh, humans.
Why have we not learned?
Where have we gone wrong?
Some have learned the truth while others ignored it.
Why?
For we are all in it together.
To be one yet intricately unique.
Be wise and take time out to relearn new strategies for it
will save your life for the next crisis.

Ignore

To ignore what's happening or to lead forward.
To ignore will cost you lives.
To ignore the hard truth about life.
To ignore because of greed and power.
For many do not have the courage to be unique.
To be brave.
To go against all stupidity and do what is best for mankind.
For life is precious.
Oh, yes life is precious beyond belief.
For its better to be brave then give into being ignorant.

Cost

How can one say that my life is less valuable than yours?
There is no value.
No comparison.
For humans should always have the choice to be free.
Yet we live in a society that is not always so.
Look around you.
For you shall see the hard truth in front of you.
For you may be free but others around you may not be.
Humans and cost of choosing.

Lost

To be lost.
To look lost.
To feel lost.
To not know which way to go.
Can only go forward.
Never backwards for that defeats the point, does it no?
But many humans live in the past for they are too afraid to
look forward.
So, they rather remain lost in their ways.
So sad.
For the future is where you become clearer within.
To feel balanced with oneself.
Try it and you will love it!

Remain

To remain in the past and the present for who knows what the future holds.

But to remain in the past is too difficult for life will continue without you.

And you do not want that for you will be moved onto the present whether you like or not.

To remain in the present without learning from the past to get to the future will also have dire consequences.

For life is always about learning.

For to evolve forward to be a better person, one must learn from the past to the present to get to the future.

For to remain otherwise, will harm you more than you can handle.

Move

Life moves on with or without you.
For life never stands still.
For life is time.
And time is life.
That energy from within.
For it's the energy that gives life.
Life that taketh or giveth life.
That energy within us.
The strength and the weakness.
That constant movement of time, energy, and life.
Oh, how wonderful it is to be alive.
That's the beauty which is all around us.

Alive

To be alive.
To see things that others don't see.
To be alive.
To feel what others don't feel.
To be one with the soul.
For the soul is all.
That energy that feels the past, present and the future.
Oh, to be alive.
For you see things that others take for granted.
You are the inspiration that gives life to others.
For they have given up or to afraid.
But not you.
For you are alive!

Understand

To understand more than you need.
To understand human nature for that is not always easy.
To understand yet not always.
For sometimes in life, it's not always explanatory.
To understand thru senses is wonderful.
For then you feel alive.
Oh, to understand the world around is tough for sometimes you don't want to be burdened.
For you feel more than others.
And that is hard.
Yet, satisfying in a way for you are open to all things around you.
Are you not?

Explain

Some things in life is unexplanatory.
Those are the times when it's the senses that take over.
For you trust with all your mind that what you see before
you is true.
For you are the truth.
The light that is needed.
You see it in others when you interact with them.
Their souls become alive.
For some things in life, one can't always explain why its
one way and not this way.
Oh, the mysteries of life.
Waiting for us to accept with openness.
So, go ahead, trust and see what happens.

Burden

To be burdened.
To take on the burden.
Means to accept all energies around oneself.
To know why you do this.
For you feel more than others.
For you want to understand each energy.
Which you do.
For you know that we are one yet unique.
You have seen things that are too hard to describe.
To feel the burden of others.
To be one with all.
What a burden.
But you are learning that not all can be saved.
Can you?
Life as a human.

Afraid

Why be afraid?
This is just a new thing that humans must go thru.
For we have become mundane in our thinking.
For we each hold the key to finding a solution.
For its inside.
We just need to learn to be open to the fact that our
knowledge resides within.
For the soul knows and waits patiently for the mind to
become one so together they can understand it.
Oh, do not be afraid for life is about learning.
Just learn to trust oneself more.

Hold

What do you hold?
Do you hold the key to mankind?
No.
We each hold the key.
For the soul is the key to the universe.
To be one with all.
To feel the energy flow thru us.
For we feel the knowledge of being awakened within.
Do you not feel it?
For as we become one within, we succumb to the
knowledge of what the universe is telling us.
So, do you hold a part of the key to mankind and maybe
more?

Succumb

To be open to other ideas.
To accept that what is happening to you is something special.
That you are one of many who are going thru this transition.
We all would be if we just accepted the impossible.
We are all able to do this.
To let go of the fear and trust with all your soul that this is who we are.
We are more than what we are led to believe.
To succumb yet being aware with all our senses and more.
For its that energy within us that sets us free.

Dream

To dream the impossible.
To be the impossible.
For you have set the standard.
That life can turn out wonderful.
To be open to all things.
Being positive no matter how hard life is.
To dream that life is possible after all.
To trust yourself that what is happening to you is for a purpose.
To be there for others as they go thru this experience.
Oh, to dream the dream of many wonderful things to come.

Passage

A passage in time.
Time in passage.
For that is life.
The experiences we go thru.
For us to evolve forward, our passage thru life helps us go forward.
Don't you agree?
Life on this planet.
One way or another will help us proceed forward.
Time.
For time flows thru each and every one of us.
A passage in which the energy flows thru us while we expand the knowledge within ourselves.

Part

To be a part of.
Why?
Often times, I wonder why I am a part of these events.
From the moment I was born till now.
Life has taken me thru many trials.
And it still continues.
I know I am being tested but it only makes me stronger.
For I believe in my soul more than ever.
Oh, to be a part of something that is much bigger than
man can imagine.

Bigger

To be bigger than life.
To be more powerful than one can imagine.
For that is the beauty of the soul.
For the soul is bigger than we ever imagined.
Its everything.
Everything that you imagined.
Its there waiting for you to accept.
For it waits patiently, each passing moment, till you
become one within.
The soul.
The giver of life and the one that taketh.
For it has one purpose, to learn so that it may evolve.
The soul.

U-turns

U-turns are great.
They help reset life.
Life decisions as well.
To save lives.
For to live is precious as it's so fragile.
Fragility.
Helps humans to see the value of things more clearly.
The U-turns.
Everyone does them.
One minute we are set in our ways and the next, new decisions.
Life as a human.
Never ends does it.
Oh, to be human yet more.

Contribute

To contribute towards society.
To give back.
To help others see the bigger picture.
To bring joy and laughter in.
To be there when others need you.
To contribute in your own unique way.
To be human yet more.
To show no fear.
To be unique for you have a knowledge like no other.
You are you, yet more.
To contribute.
How do you contribute?

Love

Love is the key.
The key that will get you thru life.
Love is what sets you free.
To be one within and more.
To love oneself.
To be bond to others.
To see things that others often times don't or can't see.
Love is the shield to get thru life.
Love is that inner strength you have inside.
Love.
To love oneself whole-heartedly is for the soul to be at its
mightiest.
That inner peace.

Deep

To dig deep.
To look deeply within you.
For the answer lies within you.
For the soul lays itself bare for all that want to be one.
All you need to do is find it.
For the answer lies within.
Look and you shall find.
Yet be patient for it takes time.
For what is time if not being patient.
Oh, to have the patience of a saint but even they must look deep within.
Thus, we can too.
So, look deep within oneself and you shall find what you are looking for.

Lies

What lies beneath my soul?
The universe.
For there lies time, space and energy.
All one yet more.
For there lies the truth.
The truth of who we are.
To believe in the impossible.
To be one with nature.
For that is the energy that flows within.
Oh, what lies within my soul?
All.
For I am the past, present and the future.
I am the light that shines in the darkness.
I am the giver of life.
I am all yet more.
Oh, what am I?

More

To be more yet less.
To be simple yet not.
To believe is the best.
To love the impossible.
To be the future for you have evolved.
To be the energy that flows thru.
To be patient with oneself.
To be fair.
To be compassionate.
To be loving.
To feel more than others.
To take the burden upon oneself.
To love will all your heart.
To be more yet not.
To be you.

Suppress

To suppress.
To be suppressed.
To suppress nature.
For nature needs air.
To be one with oneself.
The energy that flow thru.
For lately, its been crying.
As humans have not been listening to its warnings.
Humans.
For we are a part of nature, if not all.
So why suppress something that is a part of us?
For we are all inter-connected.
Lets see if we can be the opposite for nature needs us more
than ever.

live

To live.
To be alive.
To know why.
For life is about living and learning.
For to live a happy one we all should learn and
listen to our soul.
For the soul will show you the way.
But I understand that you fear the unknown.
For its not.
It's a part of you.
You know but you do not accept.
Oh, to live as a part of the soul yet more.

Defy

To defy oneself.
To go against the soul.
For the soul is always there.
Waiting.
For it wants to show something.
But the mind does not always want..
For it has other plans.
Or so it thinks.
For without the soul, there is nothing.
The energy that flows thru us that binds the two together.
So why go against the order of nature?
For they both are a part of nature yet unique.

Cease

To cease all activity.
To remain calm.
To be one with oneself.
To learn about who you are.
To be there in spirit.
For the soul welcomes you with open arms.
To be your true self.
To learn to forgive oneself of all the mistakes
that you have done.
To live and let go.
For you love yourself thru and thru.
To allow yourself to be open to the impossible for its all
possible.
You will see.
Love, peace and harmony!

Reach

To reach for the stars.
For they look so far away.
But are they?
For sometimes it looks as thou you could touch them.
What an illusion.
Makes one think, does it not?
What would you do if you could reach for a star?
Would you keep it, destroy it or let it be?
You choose.
But choose wisely.
For it will teach you the type of person you are.
Wish you well!

Hold

To hold your hand one last time.
To hold your essence always.
To hold the memory in my mind.
Yet the soul feels you all the time.
To hold.
Why do humans hold onto things that in the end
has no value?
When to hold onto something shall always be a part of you.
Don't you think?

Unknown

To be the unknown.
To not know what the future holds let alone the present.
For no one knows what will happen in an hour from now.
You may think you do but it changes.
For life is constantly changing.
Time changes.
For it fluctuates thru the unknown.
Feeling with the soul at the forefront.
For the soul knows, for it has seen the future, the present and the past.
It knows.
But it waits patiently for the mind to follow and trusting in the unknown.

Mind

What is the mind?
That organ that sits in your head.
That never sleeps.
Constantly churning thru the day's events.
Synchronizing itself with the soul.
Yet wanting to be its own master.
Always fighting.
Always demanding.
Always being annoying for it can if you let it.
But it can be taught.
Anything can be taught, can it not?
For the mind is calm and one with the soul.
But not always.
For I am still a human.
Not perfect.
Still learning.
Like we all are.

Unique

To be unique.
Do you feel unique?
You should.
For you are born.
Are intelligent.
Beautiful.
A giver.
A provider.
Unique.
To be unique in many things, even things that is unknown to us.
For one has to travel in time to find out what that is.
Oh, to be unique.
To anticipate when you must wait patiently for that is when things happen.
And not before.
Unique!

Sacrifice

Humans sacrifice themselves on a daily basis.
Humans have this great capacity of being compassionate.
Humans will do anything to save another.
Humans are giving, caring, selfless, kind, compassionate
and much more.
Humans.
To sacrifice yourself for another whether they be family or
stranger, is the greatest gift you can offer.
To be one with oneself.
For the soul will always sacrifice itself for your happiness.

Life

What is life?
Life is so precious.
Life is nature.
Nature which in turn sustains humans and everything else.
Life is the energy that surrounds us.
That keeps all things ticking.
Ticking to time.
Time which is timeless.
For that is life.
It never ends.
It flows thru all living things.
That is life.

Component

That component that holds things together.
What is that?
Do you know?
An inkling.
Its called love.
For love is what keeps the mind and the soul together.
For love is powerful.
For both, to be in balance, its that harmony, between the two.
For love heals all hate that the mind could come up with towards the soul.
Yet, the soul is always at peace for it does not want to cause harm.
Peace, love and harmony!

Both

You and I have come a long way.
We came into this world screaming and for what?
For some life is hard and others calm.
To be together thru good times and horrible times.
Learning along the way to trust each other.
That the ones who love us, may not always be honest.
To be together.
Sometimes one leaves the other because of the stress of
everyday life.
But in actual fact we are always together.
Always learning.
Learning about what makes the other who it is.
To be together.
To finally reach a stage where we can no longer afford to
be separate.
For we need each other too much.
Thank you both for loving each other.

Jigsaw

Life is like a jigsaw puzzle.
Full of missing pieces.
That one has to put together throughout one's life.
Some pieces are easy but as time expands, so do the pieces.
Some with odd shapes, some with curves, some triangular,
some hexagon, some obtuse and all other sorts.
Can you imagine using these pieces in your life?
To remember where they fit.
A life full of jigsaw.
Hopefully at the end of time, they all fit perfectly.

Potential

What is your potential?
Lots.
For we each came to earth to learn something.
Something which is not always attainable at first.
For if we knew that we would not be here, would we?
No.
For we would be somewhere else, collecting our experiences.
For each time we learn, we evolve ourselves into something better.
What's your potential?

Presence

To be in your presence.
To feel you.
To not always want to acknowledge you for fear of something.
For to acknowledge your existence means I must change my ways.
And do I?
For to be happier within my mind and knowing that the soul is always at my side.
Is to acknowledge its presence.
And that takes a lot of trust to become one yet two entities.

Fear

What do you fear?
For fear is just a by-product of society.
For society knows how to bring fear into your mind.
For it has ways to make you think that what you want the most and what to fear.
Fear.
Yet, there is nothing to fear.
For fear is just a figment of your imagination.
If you learn that fear is nothing then that, then you have managed to remove yourself and see the bigger picture that is being played at hand.

Footsteps

To follow the steps of the foot.
Wherever it may lead me.
For the future has not been foretold.
For no one knows really where the footsteps are leading
today.
You must just trust that you are going the right way.
For your path has been planned out already.
Would you not agree?
I wonder, where my footpath will lead today?
Oh, I can't wait.

Conflict

There is a conflict happening right now.
Between humans and nature.
Nature is at its limits because humans have been slowly
damaging nature.
Why?
Don't you like earth?
For what has it ever done to you.
Except claim its territory.
We would do the same, would we not?
That constant battle between man and nature.
Lets hope for our sake, nature survives.
For without, it would be sad!

Positive

Life is full of positivity.
Never give up.
Even when you are in pain.
For there are those who are always by your side.
No matter how far.
For our souls are always connected.
Always remain positive.
For there is hope and love waiting for you.
Trust with all your soul that you will be good.
Listen to your soul for the soul will help you find the peace
you need at this moment of time.

Cheerfulness

Such cheerfulness you both have.
For its nice to see you both so happy.
For life has become slightly abnormal.
Oh, to see such cheerfulness.
For it brings the mood right up.
For life is hard enough.
I see it every day.
People are beyond stress yet trying to put on a brave face.
Oh, humans, do not fear for life will be ok.
Think of cheerful things.
That will bring a smile to your face.

Frighten

I am not frightened just cautious.
I am more concerned for the well-being of others.
Those that don't have anything to keep themselves safe.
What about them?
The forgotten ones.
Who will look out for them?
To be frightened in this new age.
For why should we?
We know how to take care of ourselves.
We do it every day, do we not?
So why are you panicking?
Give a thought to the less fortunate.

Forgotten

To be forgotten.
To not exist.
It will be a trialling time.
To see the fittest versus the weakest.
But should it be?
For we have the necessary skills, do we not?
We just need common sense.
To come together as one.
Yet uniquely separate.
For we each have our own ideas.
That does not matter as long as we do not forget those you may wish to forget.
For they will never be forgotten will they.
To never forget.

Trial

What a momentous time this is.
For this is a trial of humanity coming together.
Is it not?
For humans always want to remain separate with ideas
when its these sort of crisis that we must come together and
share information.
Yet, there are those that still are keeping quiet.
Why?
What is there to gain, except death?
Human sacrifice.
Oh, humans and their trials.
All part of learning.

Risk

What's a risk?
To do something that your soul does not like.
That is the mind.
For the mind likes to take risks.
To be daring.
More like to be stupid.
What do you get out by being risky other than a broken bone or no money?
Nothing.
For the soul knows things that the mind does not.
Yet the soul is very forgiving for its patient, loving and always calm.
For it knows in the end, the mind will become one with the soul.

The author

Born in Namibia, Nicole Luck attended high school in Indonesia, completed a BA in Philosophy in the USA, and achieved an MA in Hotel and Tourism Management in London. Luck's works, based on her life experiences, touch on themes such as truth, light, love, honesty, compassion, being unique, nature, friendship, time, soul, energy, and self-esteem, among others. She enjoys travel, reading, and writing, and has previously published two other works, including *Being Unique*.

The publisher

*He who stops
getting better
stops being good.*

This is the motto of novum publishing, and our focus
is on finding new manuscripts, publishing them and
offering long-term support to the authors.
Our publishing house was founded in 1997, and since
then it has become THE expert for new authors and
has won numerous awards.

**Our editorial team will peruse each manuscript
within a few weeks free of charge and without
obligation.**

You will find more information about
novum publishing and our books on the internet:

www.novum-publishing.co.uk

Nicole Luck

Being Unique

ISBN 978-3-99107-055-9
72 pages

Get this out there as it needs to be read and spread in these troubling times! It is an inspirational message for all, that we are all precious and that we and our souls need to be protected, from birth to the humble postman and bus driver.

9 783903 861794